D1186894

party food
for kids

party food
for kids

caroline marson

photography by polly wreford
styled by rose hammick

RYLAND
PETERS
& SMALL
LONDON NEW YORK

First published in the United Kingdom
in 2007 by Ryland Peters & Small
20–21 Jockey's Fields
London WC1R 4BW
www.rylandpeters.com

10 9 8 7 6 5 4 3 2 1

Text, design and photographs
© Ryland Peters & Small 2007

ISBN: 978-1-84597-476-3

The recipes in this book were originally
published in *Children's Parties*.

All rights reserved. No part of this
publication may be reproduced, stored
in a retrieval system, or transmitted
in any form or by any means,
electronic, mechanical, photocopying
or otherwise, without the prior
permission of the publisher.

A CIP record for this book is available
from the British Library.

Printed and bound in China

Designer Jo Fernandes
Editor Ann Baggaley
Picture research Emily Westlake
Production Gemma Moules
Publishing director Alison Starling

Stylist Rose Hammick

Notes:
All spoon measurements are level
unless otherwise specified.

Recipes in this book were tested using
a regular oven. If using a fan-assisted
oven, follow the manufacturer's
instructions for adjusting
temperatures.

contents

a special feast

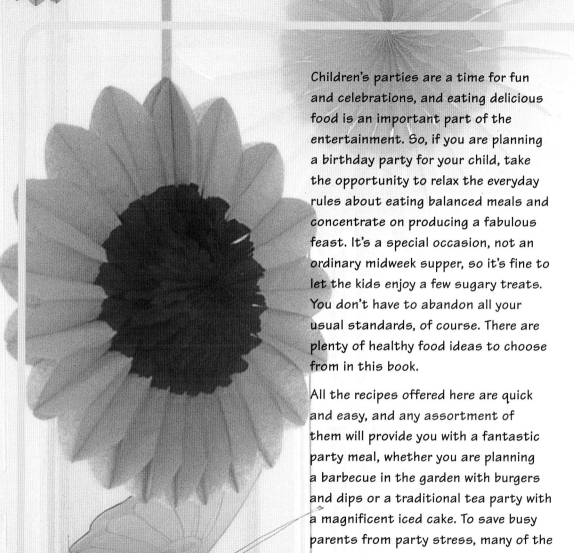

Children's parties are a time for fun and celebrations, and eating delicious food is an important part of the entertainment. So, if you are planning a birthday party for your child, take the opportunity to relax the everyday rules about eating balanced meals and concentrate on producing a fabulous feast. It's a special occasion, not an ordinary midweek supper, so it's fine to let the kids enjoy a few sugary treats. You don't have to abandon all your usual standards, of course. There are plenty of healthy food ideas to choose from in this book.

All the recipes offered here are quick and easy, and any assortment of them will provide you with a fantastic party meal, whether you are planning a barbecue in the garden with burgers and dips or a traditional tea party with a magnificent iced cake. To save busy parents from party stress, many of the recipes can be prepared in advance of the great day.

savouries

crudités and dips

Dips served with crudités, including carrot, red pepper, tomatoes, cucumber and celery, make great finger foods. Some children won't eat raw vegetables, so offer dippers such as crisps and breadsticks. These recipes serve about 8.

dippers

breadsticks, small or large

tortilla chips

beetroot, carrot and parsnip vegetable crisps

mini oat biscuits or mini rice cakes

toasted pitta bread sliced into strips

Sweet potato wedges:
Peel and cut 900 g sweet potatoes into wedges. Place them in a roasting tin, toss in a tablespoon of olive oil and sprinkle with a teaspoon of paprika. Cook for 35–40 minutes at 200°C (400°F) Gas 6, turning a few times. Serve with a sour cream dip (see below).

sour cream dip

150 ml crème fraîche

2 spring onions, finely chopped

1 tablespoon lemon juice

Lightly mix together all the ingredients. Don't over-stir, as the dip will go runny. This can be made in advance and kept in the fridge.

houmous

1 x 400-g tin organic chickpeas, drained

juice of 1 lemon

75 ml light tahini paste

2 tablespoons light olive oil, plus extra for drizzling

1 garlic clove, peeled and crushed

2 tablespoons boiling water

sea salt, to taste

Put the chickpeas and lemon juice in a blender and work to a smooth purée. Add the tahini paste, olive oil and garlic and blend until smooth. Scrape down the sides of the blender and add the boiling water. The consistency of the mixture should be fairly loose and light. Taste and adjust the seasoning with a little sea salt if necessary, spoon into bowls and drizzle with a little olive oil. The houmous will keep in the fridge for a couple of days.

kids' guacamole

2 ripe avocados, halved and diced

2 tablespoons mayonnaise

1 teaspoon finely chopped fresh coriander leaves

2 tablespoons crème fraîche

Whizz the avocado, mayonnaise and coriander together in a processor. Put in a bowl and stir in the crème fraîche. Push the avocado stones into the dip to prevent discoloration. Remove before serving. This will keep in the fridge for 1 day.

cookie-cutter sandwiches

Sandwiches cut with cookie cutters look special.
Don't make them more than 2–3 hours ahead –
they'll go soggy.

Serves 6–8

Egg mayonnaise and cress:
Mash 4 hard-boiled eggs in a bowl and
mix with 4 teaspoons mayonnaise. Divide
between 4 slices of bread, top with cress
and 4 more slices, and cut into shapes.

Banana and peanut butter:
Spread 8 slices of bread with peanut
butter. Slice 2 large bananas, place the
banana rings on 4 of the slices and cover
with the other 4 slices. Cut into shapes.

cheese straws

125 g wholemeal flour, plus extra for dusting
55 g butter, plus extra for greasing
85 g Parmesan cheese, finely grated
1 egg yolk

Makes 20 small straws
OR 10 giant straws

These taste delicious with the dips on pages 10–11, and can be cut into either giant straws or finger lengths.

Preheat the oven to 200°C (400°F) Gas 6. Lightly grease a baking sheet.

In a food processor, combine the flour and butter until the mixture resembles fine crumbs. Add two-thirds of the cheese, plus the egg and 2–3 tablespoons water, and process in bursts until the mixture forms a ball. Flatten the dough slightly, wrap in clingfilm and chill for 30 minutes.

On a floured surface, roll the dough out to about 1 cm thickness and cut into long or short strips, according to preference. Lift onto the baking sheet and sprinkle with the remaining cheese. Bake for 10 minutes or until golden. Cool on a wire rack.

pitta pockets

To freshen pitta bread, lightly sprinkle it with a little water then place in a toaster for a minute, cut it in half, and choose from one of the following filling suggestions.

All recipes fill 6–8 halves of pitta bread

Tuna and carrot salad:
Combine a drained 185 g can of tuna with 2 coarsely grated carrots, 2 tablespoons chopped flat leaf parsley and 2 tablespoons mayonnaise in a small bowl.

Cheese, bacon and tomato:
Combine 50 g coarsely grated cheddar cheese with 2 tablespoons crème fraîche, 2 chopped tomatoes and 4 rashers of crispy bacon, finely chopped.

Chicken and avocado salad:
Combine 125 g chopped chicken breast with 1 ripe avocado, 2 tablespoons crème fraîche, 1 tablespoon lemon juice, 1 tablespoon mayonnaise and 50 g cos lettuce, shredded.

garlic and herb bread

3 garlic cloves, peeled
and crushed

10 g butter, very soft

3 tablespoons olive oil

1 tablespoon chopped
fresh flat leaf parsley

1 tablespoon chopped
fresh basil leaves

4 ciabatta rolls, split in half

Makes 8 portions

This healthy but tasty recipe
uses less butter than 'normal'
garlic bread.

Preheat the oven to 200°C (400°F)
Gas 6.

Combine the garlic, butter, oil,
parsley and basil in a bowl and
whisk, mixing well, until the butter
and oil emulsify.

Spread each half-roll generously
with the butter, place the two
halves together and wrap each
roll in foil. Cook for 10–15 minutes.

If you are using a barbecue, place
the foil parcels over a medium heat
for 10 minutes, turning once.

These are delicious either eaten
on their own or served with salad.

surprise burgers

Kids will enjoy helping you squelch the burger mixture into patties. You can make and freeze these burgers ahead of the party date – just remember to defrost them well before cooking.

500 g minced beef

2 teaspoons tomato ketchup, plus extra to serve

1 tablespoon teriyaki sauce

4 spring onions, finely chopped

1 medium egg, lightly beaten

125 g Cheddar cheese, cut into 8 small pieces

flour for dusting

vegetable oil for brushing

8 small, part-baked bread rolls

8 small cos lettuce leaves

Makes 8 burgers

Mix together the mince, ketchup, sauce, spring onions and egg in a large bowl. With damp hands, divide the mixture into 8 balls, then insert a piece of cheese in the centre of each one. Wrap the meat around the cheese and shape into a burger. Place on a lightly floured plate and chill for 30 minutes.

Brush the burgers with oil and cook on a cast-iron griddle pan or under a hot grill for 5–8 minutes on each side.

Meanwhile, bake the rolls according to the packet instructions. Split them in half and top the bases with the burgers, tomato ketchup and a lettuce leaf.

If you are cooking on a barbecue, oil a barbecue griddle and cook over a medium heat (so the burgers don't burn on the outside) for 5–8 minutes each side.

finger-lickin' drumsticks

4 tablespoons tomato
ketchup

4 tablespoons
Worcestershire sauce

4 tablespoons dark
brown sugar

2 tablespoons American
mustard or Dijon mustard

8 chicken drumsticks
or 16 chicken wings

Serves 8

The marinade in this recipe is also great for pork chops or spare ribs.

For the marinade and dipping sauce, combine the ketchup, sauce, sugar and mustard in a bowl.

Put the chicken in an airtight plastic bag, pour in half the sauce, shake the bag and seal the end. Refrigerate for at least 3 hours.

Preheat the oven to 220°C (425°F) Gas 7. Remove the chicken from the bag and cook in a baking dish for about 35–40 minutes, turning the pieces occasionally.

Pour the remaining sauce into a pan, add 125 ml water and bring to the boil for 5 minutes, then pour into a small dish. Remove the chicken from the oven and cool slightly, then serve with the sauce.

If you are using a barbecue, scrape any excess marinade off the chicken. Cook over direct heat for 40 minutes, turning occasionally.

hot dog howlers

Hot dog sauce:

1 small onion, finely chopped

80 ml tomato ketchup

1 teaspoon mustard powder

1 teaspoon demerara sugar

1 teaspoon paprika (optional)

8 good-quality pork sausages

8 small milk rolls or wholemeal rolls

125 g Cheddar cheese, grated

Makes 8 hot dogs

Children love hot dogs. The sauce freezes well and can be made in advance.

In a saucepan combine all the sauce ingredients together with 250 ml water. Bring to the boil and reduce the heat. Simmer for 5–10 minutes until thick and pulpy.

In a large frying pan, cook the sausages over a very low heat for about 20 minutes, turning them every now and then, until they are cooked thoroughly.

To serve, slice the rolls lengthways. Place a sausage in each roll, and top with the sauce and a little grated cheese.

crispy new potatoes

700 g new potatoes, scrubbed

4 tablespoons olive oil

a little ground black pepper, to taste

rosemary sprigs (optional)

2 tablespoons finely grated Parmesan cheese

bamboo skewers

Serves 8

These potatoes become nicely crunchy on the outside. Children love them as a side dish.

Preheat the oven to 200°C (400°F) Gas 6.

Toss the potatoes in a roasting tin with the oil, black pepper and rosemary. Roast them in the oven for 30–35 minutes, turning occasionally. Sprinkle over the grated cheese just before serving.

If you are cooking on the barbecue, cook the potatoes in a pan of boiling water for 10–12 minutes or until tender. Drain and return to the pan with the oil, black pepper and sprigs of rosemary (if using). Thread the potatoes on bamboo skewers that have been soaked in cold water for 30 minutes. Place on the barbecue and cook over a medium heat for 7–8 minutes, turning regularly, until golden. Sprinkle over the grated cheese just before serving.

fruity coleslaw

350 g white or red cabbage, coarsely grated

1 large carrot, coarsely grated

2–3 celery sticks, finely sliced

1 red dessert apple, cored and diced

1 ripe mango, peeled and diced

150 ml mayonnaise

salt and a little ground black pepper, to taste

Serves 8

Using a food processor with a coarse grater will cut out the lengthy process of hand-grating.

Combine the grated cabbage and carrot in a large bowl with the celery, apple and mango. Add the mayonnaise and season. Toss well to mix. Cover and leave in a cool place for 2–3 hours before serving.

This coleslaw is delicious as a side dish with Finger-lickin' Drumsticks (see page 18) or eaten with Garlic and Herb Bread (see page 15). You can make it in advance of the party as it will keep in the fridge for a couple of days.

sweet treats

sticky toffee apples

12 small dessert apples
12 wooden lolly sticks
450 g demerara sugar
2 tablespoons golden syrup

60 g unsalted butter
4 teaspoons lemon juice
colourful sprinkles

Makes 12 apples

The toffee becomes soft after about 2 hours – so make these on the day of the party.

Wash and dry the apples. Remove the stalks and push a lolly stick into the middle of each one.

Line a baking sheet with oiled greaseproof paper.

Put the sugar, syrup, butter, lemon juice and 4 tablespoons water into a heavy-based saucepan. Bring to a rapid boil and, stirring all the time, boil until the mixture reaches 140°C (275°F). If you don't have a sugar thermometer, drop a teaspoon of toffee into a jug of cold water. If the toffee dissolves it's not ready, but if it becomes stringy it's ready. Take the pan off the heat and dip the base into a bowl of water to prevent the toffee from burning.

Dip the apples into the toffee until evenly coated. Stand them on the baking tray, scatter with sprinkles and leave to set in a cool dry place.

rainbow popcorn

3 tablespoons vegetable oil

115 g popcorn kernels

6 tablespoons runny honey

1 teaspoon each natural food colouring, such as beetroot, spinach and turmeric powder

50 g butter

For the cones:

wrapping paper

sticky tape

Makes about 8 cones

Popcorn can be made a day ahead if you use an airtight container to keep it crisp.

Heat 1 tablespoon of the oil in a large pan over high heat. Add a third of the corn kernels, cover and cook, shaking the pan, until all the kernels pop.

Remove from the heat and transfer the popcorn to a large bowl. In the empty saucepan, melt 2 tablespoons honey, 1 teaspoon beetroot powder and a third of the butter. Return the popped corn to the pan, toss through the coloured butter, then set aside. Repeat the process twice more, using up the remaining corn kernels, honey and butter with different coloured powders.

To serve, cut pretty wrapping paper into 30-cm squares, roll into cones and secure with sticky tape.

smoothie jellies

Using ready-made smoothies makes this recipe quick and easy.

5 sheets of leaf gelatine
700 ml fruit smoothie
summer berries, to decorate
8 individual moulds, wetted

Makes 8 jellies

Dissolve the gelatine according to the instructions on the packet, then combine with the smoothie and whisk. Pour into the moulds and transfer to the fridge to set.

To turn out, dip the moulds in warm water and invert onto plates. Decorate with the berries. The jellies will keep for 2–3 days in the fridge.

jolly jelly boats

3 large oranges

1 packet fruit-flavoured jelly

cocktail sticks

rice paper or coloured paper cut into sail shapes

Makes 12 boats

Children love these colourful little jelly boats.

Cut the oranges in half. Squeeze out the juice, taking care not to pierce the skins, and scrape out the insides of the oranges. Make up the jelly according to the packet instructions. Place the orange shells on a baking sheet and pour in the jelly mixture, making sure they are full to the top and the surface is level. Refrigerate until set.

Once set, cut the oranges into wedges, using a sharp, wet knife. Pierce the paper sails with a cocktail stick and attach a sail to each jelly boat. The orange halves can be made 2–3 days ahead of time and kept uncut in the fridge.

home-made ice lollies

When made from fruit and yoghurt, lollies can
be healthy as well as delicious. You can buy the
moulds in kitchen shops or department stores.

orange and mango ice lollies

4 large ripe mangoes, peeled, stoned
and roughly chopped
250 ml freshly squeezed orange juice

Makes 8–10 lollies

In a liquidizer, whizz the mango until
smooth. Stir in the orange juice.
Transfer the mixture to a jug, then pour
into the lolly moulds. Press on the lids
and freeze overnight.

frozen fruit and yoghurt lollies

2 x 420-g pots vanilla yoghurt
1 x 300-g bag frozen mixed berries
2 tablespoons honey

Makes 8–10 lollies

In a liquidizer, whizz the yoghurt,
mixed berries and honey until smooth.
Transfer the mixture to a jug, then pour
into the lolly moulds. Press on the lids
and freeze overnight.

sparkling elderflower ices

500 ml sparkling mineral water
100 ml elderflower cordial

Makes 12 small lollies

In a large jug, mix the water with
the cordial and stir until the cordial
dissolves. Pour into the lolly moulds,
press on the lids and freeze overnight.

knickerbocker glories

A tower of jelly and ice cream topped with a fizzing sparkler is the perfect end to any birthday meal.

1 packet strawberry jelly
1 packet lemon jelly
1 x 200-g tin peaches, or 4 ripe peaches
1 x 200-g tin pineapple, or 1 pineapple
1 x 500-ml tub vanilla ice cream
140 ml double cream, lightly whipped
8 fresh cherries, to decorate
indoor sparklers

Makes 8 sundaes

Make up the jellies according to the packet instructions; pour into shallow containers lined with clingfilm, cool, then refrigerate until set.

Chop the fruit into small chunks and divide it between 8 glasses. Turn out the jellies and roughly chop them. Add layers of jelly to each glass, then a scoop of ice cream. Top with whipped cream, a cherry and a sparkler. Tell the children to stand well back until the sparkler has gone out.

Thread 3 fruit pieces onto each cocktail stick, chill and serve with the dips.

Winter fruit version:

1 small pineapple, peeled, cored and cut into chunks

1 mango, peeled, stoned and cut into small chunks

2 bananas, peeled and cut into small chunks

Summer fruit version:

125 g strawberries, hulled

2 peaches, halved, stoned and cut into chunks

1 small cantaloupe melon, skin removed, deseeded and cut into small chunks

Sweet dips:

Greek yoghurt and honey, mixed to taste

225 g milk chocolate melted with 1 tablespoon golden syrup

hundreds and thousands

cocktail sticks

Makes 8 kebabs

mini fruit fondue

You can make the sauces in advance – they will keep in the fridge for 2 days. The fruit kebabs can be assembled quickly just before you need them.

strawberry apple slush puppy

500 g strawberries, hulled
500 ml chilled apple juice
juice of 2 limes or lemons
2 tablespoons caster sugar
crushed ice
1 litre chilled soda water (optional)
strawberries, to decorate

Makes 8 glasses

In a blender, process the strawberries,
fruit juices, sugar and ice to a slush.
Pour into glasses, top with soda water
and a strawberry, and serve at once.

fruity cocktails

The essential features of any children's cocktail
are a catchy name, vivid colour and accessories
like bendy straws, cocktail umbrellas and fruit.

Makes 8 glasses

lemon silver bullet

4 unwaxed lemons
1.5 litres boiling water
4–6 tablespoons honey
1 litre chilled soda water
crushed ice
lemon and lime slices, to decorate

Coarsely grate the rind of each lemon,
add the rind to the boiling water in a
pan and simmer gently for 5–6 minutes.

Meanwhile, squeeze the lemons. Add the
lemon juice, and honey to taste, to the
pan. Stir until dissolved and pour into a
jug. When cool, strain the drink into a
clean bottle and discard the rind. Check
for sweetness. Chill until ready to serve.
To serve, fill each glass two-thirds full
with the drink and top with soda water,
crushed ice and lemon or lime slices.

tropical punch

175 g sugar cubes
175 ml boiling water
200 g ripe mango or melon, peeled,
deseeded and chopped
juice of 2 limes and 2 lemons
500 ml chilled orange or
pineapple juice
500 ml sparkling mineral water
ice cubes, to serve

Stir the sugar and water together in
a pan until the sugar has dissolved.
Set aside to cool.

Whizz the mango or melon in a blender
until smooth. Pour into a jug with the
sugar syrup and lime and lemon juices.
Stir in the orange or pineapple juice and
chill. Top with mineral water and serve
in glasses half-filled with ice cubes.

cookies & small cakes

chocolate hearts

200 g rich tea biscuits

130 g butter

3 tablespoons golden syrup

2 tablespoons cocoa powder

50 g raisins

50 g hazelnuts, toasted, skinned and roughly chopped (optional)

100 g milk chocolate

sugar flowers or icing sugar, to decorate

Makes 8–10 hearts

These biscuits need no baking. They keep for up to a week in the fridge and freeze well too.

Butter a 20-cm square tin.

Seal the biscuits in a plastic bag and smash into uneven crumbs with a rolling pin.

Melt the butter and syrup in a large pan. Stir in the cocoa powder, raisins and hazelnuts (if using), and finally the biscuit crumbs. Spoon the mixture into the tin, pressing down firmly. Melt the chocolate in a heatproof bowl over a pan of simmering water. Spread it evenly over the biscuit base and chill for 1 hour. Cut into hearts or squares to serve.

Decorate with little pink sugar flowers or icing sugar.

choc-nut flapjacks

125 g butter
125 g unrefined natural muscovado sugar
80 g golden syrup
210 g porridge oats
25 g desiccated coconut

30 g whole almonds chopped into large chunks (optional)
glacé cherries (optional)
40 g milk chocolate, roughly chopped

Makes 12 flapjacks

These flapjacks, studded with nuts and chocolate, will keep for 4–5 days in an airtight container.

Preheat the oven to 180°C (350°F) Gas 4. Lightly butter a 23-cm square cake tin and line the base.

Put the butter, sugar and golden syrup in a pan over low heat until the butter has melted and the sugar has dissolved.

Remove from the heat and stir in the oats and coconut. Spoon into the tin and press down evenly.

Scatter over the almonds and cherries (if using), and press lightly into the mixture. Bake for 15–20 minutes. Remove from the oven and immediately sprinkle over the roughly chopped chocolate. Set aside until cool.

Mark into bars or squares with a knife while still warm, then allow to cool before cutting through and removing the flapjacks from the tin.

jewel cookies

140 g butter, room temperature

100 g natural, unrefined icing sugar

1 drop vanilla extract

1 egg yolk

200 g plain flour, plus extra for dusting

30 g ground almonds (optional)

15 coloured boiled sweets

2 non-stick baking sheets, greased

Makes 20 cookies

Using a hand whisk, beat together the butter, sugar and vanilla until creamy. Add the egg yolk and beat well. Stir in the flour and ground almonds (if using) and quickly mix to a firm dough using your hands. Knead into a fat disc, wrap in clingfilm and refrigerate for 2 hours.

Divide the sweets by colour, place each colour in a plastic freezer bag and seal. Using a rolling pin, smash the sweets into tiny pieces.

Preheat the oven to 180°C (350°F) Gas 4.

On a lightly floured surface roll out the dough to a thickness of 5 mm. With cookie cutters, cut into 7-cm shapes. Cut out patterns in the centre of each cookie, leaving a generous margin. Put on the baking sheets and fill each hole with one colour of crushed sweets.

Bake for 8 minutes, or until golden brown. Remove from the oven and leave for 1 minute, then remove with a palette knife onto a wire rack.

star cookies

A sophisticated version of the jewel cookies opposite. Edible silver leaf is available from specialist cookware suppliers.

sheets of edible silver leaf

Makes 20 cookies

Follow the recipe (omitting the boiled sweets) for the jewel cookies on the opposite page, cutting the rolled-out pastry into stars with a cookie cutter. After baking, use a paintbrush to lightly dampen the surface of the cookies with cool water. When the dampened area feels tacky, use tweezers to transfer pieces of silver leaf onto the star cookies to create a mottled silver effect.

gingerbread animals

Your kids can help cut out and decorate these cute cookies. They will keep for up to a week in an airtight container.

225 g plain flour, plus extra for dusting

1 teaspoon ground ginger

1 teaspoon ground cinnamon

1 teaspoon bicarbonate of soda

60 g butter

2 tablespoons unrefined
dark brown sugar

80 g golden syrup

1 tablespoon beaten egg

icing sugar, coloured sugar, and
hundreds and thousands to decorate

Makes 25 cookies

Note: if you don't have time to make your own cookies, decorate some shop-bought gingerbread men instead — it's easy to give them fun 'clothes' with icing sugar and coloured sprinkles.

Preheat the oven to 190°C (375°F) Gas 5. Cover two baking sheets with greaseproof paper.

Blend the flour, ginger, cinnamon and bicarbonate of soda in a food processor. Add the butter and whizz until the mixture resembles fine breadcrumbs. Add the sugar, syrup and egg and blitz to form a soft dough.

Roll out the dough to 5 mm thickness. Cut out the animal shapes with cookie cutters, put them on the baking sheets and bake for 8–10 minutes until golden brown. When firm, put them on a rack to cool. To decorate, beat 2 tablespoons icing sugar with a little water to make a thin icing. Brush over the top of the cookies and sprinkle with hundreds and thousands or coloured sugar.

honey flake crunchies

15 g butter
1 tablespoon runny honey
1 tablespoon demerara sugar

30 g cornflakes
40 g sultanas

Makes 18 crunchies

Kids adore these. They will freeze or keep for up to a week in an airtight container.

Preheat the oven to 180°C (350°F) Gas 4. Line a muffin tray with 18 paper cases.

Melt the butter, honey and sugar in a small pan and stir over the heat until the butter has melted.

Add the cornflakes and sultanas and mix well. Using a tablespoon, divide the mixture between the paper cases.

Bake for 8–10 minutes or until lightly browned, remove from the oven and leave to cool.

rocky road

These are full of forbidden treats, but wow do they taste good!

Makes 18 cases

2 peanut or toffee chocolate bars, coarsely chopped

100 g small white marshmallows

70 g crisped rice cereal

75 g roasted peanuts, unsalted

200 g milk chocolate

1 teaspoon vegetable oil

Line a muffin tray with 18 paper cases.

Mix the chocolate bars, marshmallows, cereal and nuts in a bowl. Melt the milk chocolate and oil in a pan over low heat. Allow to cool slightly then stir into the other ingredients. Spoon the mix into the paper cases. Chill for 30 minutes.

butterfly cakes

These light cakes have a delicious cream-cheese icing. Make them ahead and store them in an airtight container. They freeze well undecorated.

1 tablespoon milk

3 medium eggs, lightly beaten

100 g caster sugar

115 g self-raising flour

85 g butter, melted

Cream-cheese icing:

150 g low-fat cream cheese

100 g unrefined natural icing sugar

zest of 1 unwaxed lemon or orange, plus 2 tablespoons juice

cake sprinkles and hundreds and thousands to decorate

Makes 15 cakes

Preheat the oven to 190°C (375°F) Gas 5. Line a muffin tray with 15 paper cases.

Whisk the milk, eggs and sugar in a bowl until doubled in bulk (the mix should leave a trail if the whisk is lifted). Add half the flour and half the butter and fold until evenly distributed. Fold in the remaining flour and butter. Spoon the mix into the cases, filling them almost to the top. Bake for 10 minutes until risen and golden. Cool on a wire rack.

For the icing, beat together the cream cheese, icing sugar, zest and juice of the orange or lemon until smooth.

When the cakes are cool, slice a small circle off the top of each and cut it in half. Fill the hole with cream-cheese icing and push in the two halves to form a butterfly. Decorate with sprinkles.

mini fun cakes

These little cakes are a great alternative to a traditional birthday cake. Ice them to tie in with the party's theme.

1 x 6-egg quantity of Madeira cake
(see page 52)

2 x quantity of sugar icing
(see page 55)

food colouring (optional)

icing pens in a variety of colours

Makes 25 mini cakes

Make a 25-cm square Madeira cake (see method on page 52).

When the cake has cooled, cut it across and down into 25 small squares, each measuring approximately 5 x 5 cm.

Make the sugar icing and colour it with the food colouring of your choice. Spread out the cake squares on a chopping board or cake board and pour the icing over them, covering each one completely (make sure the icing is not too runny, or this will get very messy).

When the icing has set firm, place each mini cake in a paper case. Using squeezy icing pens (available from specialist cookware suppliers), decorate each mini cake with motifs that relate to the theme of your party. The ones shown here have seaside motifs.

Arrange the cakes on a plate to form a large square.

If you are short of time, these mini cakes are easy to make from bought Madeira cake sliced up into smaller squares.

birthday cakes

victoria sandwich

175 g butter, softened
175 g naturally refined caster sugar
3 large eggs, beaten
175 g self-raising flour

This classic cake recipe is perfect if you want a traditional circular, layered party cake. Decorate as simply or lavishly as you wish.

Preheat the oven to 190°C (375°F) Gas 5. Grease and line two 18-cm sandwich tins.

Beat the butter and sugar together in a bowl until pale and fluffy. Add the eggs, a little at a time, beating in well. Fold in half the flour, using a large metal spoon, then fold in the remainder.

Divide the mixture between the tins and level the top with a palette knife. Bake in the centre of the oven for 20 minutes, or until the cakes have risen and spring back when lightly pressed in the centre. Loosen the edges of the cakes with a palette knife and leave in the tins for 5 minutes.

Turn out, remove the lining paper, invert and leave to cool on a wire rack. Sandwich the cakes together with buttercream (see page 55). Make up the sugar icing for the top (see page 55). Pour the icing over the cake and decorate with dolly mixture, or other sweeties, and candles.

Variations:
Chocolate sandwich cake: Replace 45 g flour with the same amount of cocoa powder. Sandwich the cakes together with vanilla or chocolate buttercream (see page 55).

Citrus sandwich cake: Add the finely grated zest of 1 unwaxed orange or lemon to the mixture. Sandwich the cakes together with orange or lemon buttercream (see page 55).

Coffee sandwich cake: Blend 1 teaspoon instant coffee granules with 1 tablespoon boiling water. Cool and add to the creamed mixture with the eggs. Sandwich the cakes with vanilla or coffee buttercream (see page 55).

madeira cake

Firm and moist, Madeira cake is perfect for cutting and shaping. The chart below shows quantities for making cakes of 3 different sizes.

Bakeware	25-cm square	30 x 23 cm	20-cm round
Self-raising flour	375 g	315 g	250 g
Plain flour	185 g	155 g	125 g
Butter, softened	375 g	315 g	250 g
Caster sugar	375 g	315 g	250 g
Large eggs	6 eggs	5 eggs	4 eggs
Baking time	1 hr	45 mins	50 mins

Preheat the oven to 180°C (350°F) Gas 4.

Grease and line your cake tin.

Sieve together the flours. Beat the butter and the sugar in a bowl until the mixture is pale and fluffy. Add the eggs gradually, alternating with 4 tablespoons of flour, until the mixture is light and fluffy. Add any flavouring at this point. With a large spoon, fold in the remaining flour.

Spoon the mixture into the tin, making a dip in the top with the back of the spoon. Bake in the centre of the oven for the appropriate time, until a skewer inserted in the centre comes out cleanly. Leave to cool for 10 minutes, then turn out and let the cake cool on a wire rack.

Madeira cake flavourings:
Vanilla: Add 1 teaspoon vanilla extract.

Lemon or orange: Add the grated zest and juice of 1 unwaxed lemon or 1 orange.

Chocolate: Add 2–3 tablespoons cocoa powder mixed with 1 tablespoon milk.

Almond: Add 1 teaspoon almond extract and 2–3 tablespoons ground almonds.

toppings and fillings

buttercream icing

125 g butter, room temperature

1 tablespoon milk

375 g naturally refined
icing sugar, sifted

Makes about 450 g

Thick buttercream icing hides all sorts
of sins, from burnt edges to sagging
middles. And, of course, for kids the
icing is the best bit of the cake.

Place the butter in a mixing bowl or food
processor. Add the milk and/or flavouring.
Sift the icing sugar into the bowl, a little
at a time, beating after each addition,
until all the sugar has been incorporated
and the mix is light, fluffy and smooth.

Buttercream flavourings:
Vanilla: Add 1 teaspoon vanilla extract.

Lemon or orange: Add the zest of
1 unwaxed lemon or 1 orange. Replace the
milk with 2 tablespoons freshly squeezed
lemon juice or orange juice.

Coffee: Mix the milk and 1 tablespoon
instant coffee powder to a paste and add
to the buttercream.

Chocolate: Mix the milk and 2 tablespoons

cocoa powder to a smooth paste, and add
to the buttercream.

other great cake toppings:

Sugar icing: Mix 225 g sieved icing sugar
with 2–4 tablespoons of hot water. Work
to the consistency of thin cream. Quickly
pour over cakes or cookies before it sets.

Lemon drizzle topping: Mix 115 g caster
sugar with the juice of 1 lemon, stir until
the sugar begins to dissolve, then pour
over a freshly cooked cake.

Golden meringue frosting: Put 175 g icing
sugar, 1 egg white, a pinch of cream of
tartar and 2 tablespoons hot water in
a bowl set over a pan of simmering water.
Beat with an electric whisk for 10 minutes.

palace of dreams

3 x 5-egg quantity Madeira cake
(see page 52)

2 x 450-g quantity buttercream
icing (see page 55)

5 ice-cream cones

food colouring of choice

mini sweets such as dolly mixture

rice paper or coloured paper for flags

cocktail sticks

Perfect for a birthday princess! Use
sliced Madeira cake as building blocks,
cemented with buttercream. You can
make this the day before the party.

Preheat the oven to 180°C (350°F) Gas 4.

Cook two quantities of Madeira cake in
two 30 x 23-cm greased and lined Swiss
roll tins. These two cakes form the base
of the palace. Cook one quantity of
Madeira cake in a 25-cm greased and
base-lined square tin. When cool, cut
this cake into five large squares and five
smaller ones to form the palace turrets.

Colour two-thirds of the buttercream
with food colouring of your choice and
the remainder in another colour.

To assemble: Trim the edges of the two
large rectangular cakes, then stack one

on top of the other on a large cake
board, 'glueing' the cakes together
with buttercream.

Ice the base with the larger portion of
coloured buttercream (blue in the photo).
Position one large square on each corner
and one in the centre at the back, and ice
them also with blue buttercream.

Ice the small squares with buttercream in
the second colour (pink in the photo) and
place on top of the larger squares. Top
each turret with an upturned ice-cream
cone and a cocktail-stick flag. Decorate
the whole cake with mini sweets.

gingerbread house

1 x 6-egg quantity Madeira cake
(see page 52)

2 x 450-g quantity vanilla
buttercream icing (see page 55)

1 x quantity gingerbread mixture
(see page 41)

chocolate buttons, sweets,
sprinkles, hundreds and thousands,
bought gingerbread men,
marshmallow wafers and chocolate
roll wafers to decorate

Make the cake and gingerbread ahead
of time. The house can be easily
assembled and decorated on the
morning of the party.

Make a 25-cm square Madeira cake
(see method page 52).

Trim the crust from the cake and slice
the top flat. Cut the cake into four
equal-sized squares and stack one on
top of the other, making sure each layer
is straight. Sandwich them together with
buttercream. Trim a wedge from either
side of the two top layers of cake to
create a sloping roof effect.

Preheat the oven to 190°C (375°F) Gas 5.
Measure the sides of the cake, roll out
half the gingerbread dough, and cut it to
the same dimensions. Roll out the

remaining gingerbread dough and cut two
sides for the roof. Place the gingerbread
pieces on baking sheets and bake for
10–15 minutes. Remove from the oven and
place on a wire rack to cool.

To assemble: Trim the gingerbread to fit
the sides and roof of the house. Spread a
thick layer of buttercream over the whole
cake and press the gingerbread in place.

Use the remaining buttercream to cover
the roof, so it looks as though it is snow-
covered. Decorate the house using wafers,
chocolate buttons, gingerbread men and
any little sweets or sprinkles you choose.

choo-choo train

3 shop-bought Madeira cake loaves

2 x 450-g quantity buttercream icing (see page 55)

food colouring of choice

sugar paste icing

tubes of different-coloured icing

small sweets, chocolate buttons and liquorice wheels to decorate

This impressive train was made from shop-bought cakes. You can decorate it how you like with sweets and small accessories, such as drinking straws.

Constructing a birthday cake from bought Madeira cakes couldn't be easier. Simply cut them up and use them like building blocks to create the desired shape.

To make this train, one cake was cut into thick slices to create the foundation of the train. The back of the engine was carved from one whole cake, while the rounded front of the engine was carved from the other. The pieces of cake were glued together with apricot jam. If you are working on a more elaborate structure, you may need to use wooden skewers to hold the cake together; but don't forget to remove them before slicing the cake.

Decorate the cake with a thick layer of buttercream icing. If you wish to use several different colours of icing, divide the buttercream between two or three bowls and add the desired food colouring.

For the roof of the engine, roll out the sugar paste and cut to size. Using icing tubes, add window and door outlines and any other details you desire, then decorate using sweeties, chocolate buttons and liquorice wheels.

space shuttle

1 x 4-egg quantity Madeira cake
(see page 52)

1 x 450-g quantity buttercream
icing (see page 55)

4 or 5 shop-bought mini
sponge rolls

6 ice-cream cones

red and blue Smarties, silver balls
and liquorice wheels to decorate

orange or yellow sugar paste

Send everyone to the moon in this
space shuttle. It can be assembled and
decorated the day before the party, as
long as you keep it in a cool place.

Cook the Madeira cake mixture in a
greased 1.2-litre ovenproof bowl for
50–55 minutes (see method page 52).
Turn out carefully on to a wire rack and
leave to cool.

Trim the crust from the cake and slice the
top flat. This will create the base of the
spaceship.

To assemble: Using buttercream, stick
together the mini sponge rolls. These
will form the middle part of the space
shuttle. Place them on top of the base,
then stick an upturned ice-cream cone on

top of them to form the nose cone. Cover
the whole assemblage with the remaining
buttercream icing.

Place the cake on a round cake board
and stick five ice-cream cones around
the base to form the space shuttle 'legs'.
Decorate the spaceship using blue and red
Smarties, silver balls and liquorice wheels
for portholes.

Roll out the orange sugar paste and cut
into little triangles. Stick these around
the base of the rocket and up around the
sides to create a flame effect.

index and credits

All photographs by Polly Wreford,
styled by Rose Hammick

Costumes by Maggie Bulman (020 8693 9733,
www.enchantedcastle.co.uk), pages 1 & 35 (bear),
19, 29 & 31 (mermaid), 47 (octopus)

Costumes by Rachel Causer (020 7639 8506)
pages 9 (Native American girl and cowgirl),
23 (flapper), 29 (paper mermaid hair), 49 (sheriff)

Page 8 wigwam from The Great Little Trading
Company (www.gltc.co.uk), 48 sheriff's hut from
Win Green (www.wingreen.co.uk)